WATER HOLE

Wildlife of the Tropical Dry Forest

1) Raintree
2) Yellow-headed Amazon
3) Guanacaste tree
4) Orange-chinned parakeet
5) Orange-fronted parakeet
6) Tabebuia tree
7) Fig tree
8) Stemmadenia tree
9) Scissor-tailed Flycatcher
10) Pochote tree
11) Spider monkey
12) Coati
13) Stinking toe tree
14) Elegant trogon
15) Wild Pitahaya
16) Hawk moth
17) Peanut-headed bug
18) Bromeliad
19) Boa constrictor
20) Chicle tree
21) Scrub Euphonia
22) Vine
23) Memphis butterfly
24) Prehensile-tailed porcupine
25) Sloanea tree
26) Howler monkey
27) Common ground dove
28) Monkey plum tree
29) Silky yellow-flower tree
30) Variegated squirrel
31) Magpie jay
32) Cactus
33) Gliricidia tree
34) Paper wasp
35) Coyote
36) Sandpaper tree
37) Roadside hawk
38) Charaxinae butterfly
39) Plumeria tree
40) Damselfly
41) Easter orchid
42) Sphinx moth caterpillar
43) Carpenter bee
44) Bromeliad
45) Woody opossum
46) Vine
47) Puma
48) Nine-banded armadillo
49) Marpesia butterfly
50) Hooded skunk
51) Baird's tapir, juvenile
52) White-tailed deer
53) Turquoise-browed motmot
54) Cream owl butterfly
55) Lesser Short-tailed fruit bat
56) Pauraque
57) Tropical rattlesnake
58) Collared peccary
59) Wild pineapple
60) Ant Acacia tree
61) Rufous-naped wren
62) Jamaican fruit bat
63) Climbing fern
64) Rothschildia moth
65) Scorpion
66) Scaly-breasted hummingbird
67) Gray-necked Wood Rail
68) Pelidnota beetle
69) Leaf-cutter ant
70) Ctenosaur
71) Shelf fungus
72) Guanacaste tree fruit
73) Gumbo limbo tree
74) Piper
75) Vine snake
76) Spiny pocket mouse
77) Helicteres
78) Pithecoctenium pod
79) Anole lizard
80) Agouti

WATER HOLE

LIFE IN A RESCUED TROPICAL FOREST
Kenneth Mallory

Endangered Habitats
A New England Aquarium Book

FRANKLIN WATTS
New York • Chicago • London • Toronto • Sydney

Acknowledgments

The author wishes to thank Margaret Thompson for her photographer's eyes and spirit of adventure; Patricia Fiorelli for the peccary alert; John Dayton and Richard Duggan for companionship and good will; Frank Joyce, Eric Olson, and Tom Langen for their support in the field and through the mail; Lyle Sowls and John Kaufmann for their help in understanding peccary and coati behavior; and Bob McCord, Alejandro Marin, and the staff of Santa Rosa National Park. Thanks are also due to Les Kaufman, chief scientist at the New England Aquarium, for his support of the project; Cynthia Mackey and Sandra Goldfarb, director of marketing and associate director of public relations and media programs, respectively, for their help in building a publishing program at the New England Aquarium. Thanks too to the Aquarium's supporters at Franklin Watts: former president of Franklin Watts, Richard Casabonne, former editorial director Jeanne Vestal, and my current editor Lorna Greenberg. And last and most important, special thanks to Dan Janzen, without whom this book, and the rebirth of the tropical dry forest, would never have been possible.

Library of Congress Cataloging-in-Publication Data

Mallory, Kenneth
Water hole : life in a rescued tropical forest / Ken Mallory.
p.   cm.
''A New England Aquarium book.''
Includes bibliographical references and index.
Summary: Examines the world of a tropical dry forest in Santa Rosa
National Park in Costa Rica and the work being done to preserve it.
ISBN 0-531-11154-7 (lib. bdg.). — ISBN 0-531-15250-2 (trade ed.)
1. Forest ecology—Costa Rica Parque National Santa Rosa—
Juvenile literature.   2. Forest conservation—Costa Rica—Parque
Nacional Santa Rosa—Juvenile literature.   [1. Forest ecology-
Costa Rica.   2. Forest conservation—Costa Rica.   3. Ecology—Costa
Rica.]   I. Title.
QH108.CBM35 1992
574.5'2642'097286—dc20   92–14360 CIP AC

Ten thousand years ago, a forest of evergreen and deciduous trees stretched the length of the hot Pacific lowlands of Central America. Like the rain forests that spread over the land along the Atlantic Coast, this forest—a tropical dry forest—was wet and lush for six months of the year. But unlike the rain forest, it had a desert-like dry season the other half of the year.

Strange creatures prowled the tropical dry forests in search of giant seed pods to eat. Some of the animals were called gomphotheres. They looked like the elephants of Africa today. Some were giant ground sloths—relatives of today's furry, monkey-sized sloths that live in trees, but as large as elephants. Others were cousins of the bony-plated armadillo and of the horse.

As they roamed the forests, the big animals consumed fruits and vegetation. They also were helping the forest grow. When they devoured fruits that had fallen from the trees, they often swallowed large seeds whole instead of chewing them up or spitting them out. They moved on to new areas where they deposited the undigested seeds in their dung. The seeds took root in the soil and grew into new trees, and these new trees in time created new forests.

Today these strange creatures have disappeared. Farmers and cattle ranchers have cut down most of the tropical dry forest. Small clusters of the remaining wild animals cling to what's left of their disappearing home.

In many places around the world, the forest and its residents would simply vanish from the face of the earth. But in the remarkable country of Costa Rica, the size of West Virginia, and in a unique national park called Santa Rosa, the size of San Francisco, California, the story does not end in the usual way. The story of this tropical dry forest is just beginning.

Water Hole is a glimpse into a world that is being rescued. From the water source, at the heart of the dry forest, all life in this fragile, endangered environment is visible. A group of conservation biologists and park administrators have set out to reclaim the land from farmers and ranchers and recreate the wild forest. Through the efforts of the Costa Rican government, the park administration, international donors, and Dan Janzen, a North American scientist from the University of Pennsylvania, this forest of unique plants and animals has been brought back from the edge of extinction.

EARLY MORNING OF THE DRY SEAS●N

Quebrada El Duende
(THE TROLL'S CREEK) **Water Hole**

It is six o'clock on a February morning in Santa Rosa National Park, Costa Rica, after two months without rain. A small group of coatis are sleeping, curled high above the ground in the branches of a fig tree. Coatis are relatives of the raccoon. They have long, white-tipped snouts that they use to sniff through forest leaf litter for lizards, insects, spiders, and fruits. A circle of white hairs surrounds their eyes so they look as if they are wearing masks. They use their sharp-clawed paws to climb up into the safety of trees to pick fruit, from the branches, and to dig for food.

A mother coati is the first awake. Asleep next to it are its three children, one female and two males, each about two years old. Coatis travel in bands—usually of four to twenty animals—made up of adult females and their young. Sleeping in the crotch of another branch of the tree are the other members of this band—another female coati, its two-year-old daughter, and a third adult female with no offspring of its own. One by one the three adult and four juvenile coatis begin to stir.

Coatis move easily along the branches and limbs of trees, gripping the surfaces with their sharp claws.

Aside from the white mass of hair around its snout and shoulders, the color of a coati's coat changes when it molts, from a dark brown to a red or yellow hue.

From the coatis' high perch in the fig tree, there is a clear view of a small permanent pool of water at the bottom of a natural depression lined with boulders and rocks. Other animals are already up and about. Down in this valley of stones, a troop of white-faced monkeys huddle in the early morning sun. Their faces, one atop another, form a pink and white wall. While the coatis watch, one monkey climbs up a neighbor's back. Its front paw covers its companion's eyes. It looks, it listens, and at last it runs—down to the water hole, down to quench its nagging thirst.

Once the first monkey breaks from the pack, all the rest scamper down to follow. Seven monkeys chatter and splash water everywhere. Some slurp noisily. Others cup one paw, scoop a precious handful and let trickles of water drip into their upturned mouths. Sometimes a sound from the forest disturbs them and they race back up the rocks framing the water hole. But their thirst soon brings them back for more.

A female coati tends its band of five youngsters (two are on the
ground below) as they set out to hunt for food.

A troop of white-faced (capuchin) monkeys and a swarm of bees
compete for space at the puddle-sized water hole.

7

The pool of water—the water hole—looks like a puddle, merely the length of two human footprints. Fortunately for the forest animals, however, this puddle doesn't dry up. It is like the pocket of water that appears at the bottom of a pit dug at a sandy beach. If the pit is deep enough, the water keeps returning no matter how much is removed. The monkeys drink and drink and splash water everywhere until it seems as if there could be none left. But when other thirsty animals arrive, the water miraculously returns. A hidden underground spring provides an endless supply.

As the satisfied monkeys scamper off through the trees, the coatis can move in for their turn to drink. One by one they climb down the tree, headfirst, using sharp, curved claws on their rear paws to prevent them from falling. Coatis share water holes with other animals of the forest, especially in the dry season. But this morning, at least for the time being, they have the water hole to themselves.

The mother of the three young coatis reaches the ground first, stops for a moment and raises its long snout to sniff the air. It bobs its head up and down

A white-faced monkey lets scooped-up water drip into its mouth.

Alarmed by a sound in the forest, two white-faced monkeys scamper up onto rocks and listen. Three species of monkeys live in Santa Rosa National Park: white-faced, spider, and howler monkeys.

After climbing down from a nearby fig tree, an adult female coati surveys the water hole—sniffing and listening for possible danger.

to fill its nostrils and help it sniff. The coatis' keen sense of smell helps them find tasty insects hiding under leaves, and also helps them sense the presence of danger. Predators—especially wild cats like the puma and, occasionally, large snakes—might be lurking nearby. Certain that the water hole is safe, the coatis scurry over the rocks to get their first drink of the day.

Before they can reach their goal, though, the coatis have to deal with a giant toad that has plunked itself down right in the middle of the water. Despite the approaching coatis, the pleasure of a refreshing bath is irresistible. And what a bath! This sapo grande (the Spanish words for "large toad") is in toad heaven. Almost every kind of animal and insect in the forest passes here, sometimes several times a day. So when flies, wasps, and bees swoop in for a drink, out darts sapo grande's immense and sticky tongue to gather in a meal.

Two female coatis and two youngsters, between one and two years old, visit the water hole. Coati bands are usually made up of females and young coatis like these. Scientists believe most of the females in a band may be related.

A marine toad ("sapo grande" in Spanish) squats in the center of the water hole. If the bees and wasps resting on its back are not quick enough, they may be the toad's next meal.

The toad will eat just about anything that fits in its mouth, although its usual diet is made up of beetles and ants.

Because the toad lives next to the water hole, and can spend the hot part of the day half-submerged, it is one tropical-dry-forest animal that doesn't seem to suffer from the heat. But once it senses the impatient band of coatis, the toad gives up its favored spot. It hops up under a nearby overhanging rock and waits for the intruders to leave. The toad can defend itself, if threatened, with poison from large glands on both sides of its neck. If the toad is seized in another animal's mouth, poison oozes from these glands to discourage the predator.

Now it is the coatis' turn at the water hole. The mothers and young move quietly over the rocks, tails held erect. They crouch down at the water's edge and extend their snouts to sip from the pool like feeders at a trough. Above the drinking coatis, doves flutter through the trees with mournful coos. A solitary morpho butterfly lands on a fallen tree trunk. Its striking blue color, hidden except when it flies, gleams against the dried and brown leaves covering the forest floor.

With long tails held high, two female coatis quench their thirst. Adult coatis range from 1.5 to 2.3 feet long, with tails up to 2 feet in length. ●

Although the blue morpho butterfly is rarely seen in Santa Rosa during the dry season, solitary specimens are occasionally found near river bottoms. The blue is visible only when the butterfly is flying, or flapping its wings.

This morning visit to a water hole is one of many water stops the coatis will make during the day. They have drunk their fill, but are not yet ready to move off into the forest in search of food. First they climb up onto a thick overhanging branch to groom themselves. With its youngster's back facing it, a mother coati uses its teeth to comb through the fur and remove any insects hiding there.

The coatis work hard at grooming, and they are not finished when the first of a line of slow-moving creatures appears at the top of a ravine of rocks overlooking the water hole. These are collared peccaries, distant relatives of the pig. With disklike snouts and coarse, bristly hair, they resemble small North American farm hogs. A thin stripe of gray-white fur circles below their necks like necklaces. When peccaries are alarmed, as they seem to be now, their black and brown fur stands up like that of frightened dogs or cats.

First there are grunts and clackings of teeth; and then a powerful odor. The smell—sharp, musky, and more unfamiliar than unpleasant—comes from a musk gland on the peccary's back. Peccaries secrete musk from this gland to mark territories and to help keep a social group together. The coatis seem content to let the peccaries socialize on their own.

14

As the peccaries settle in, one opens its mouth in a gaping yawn, revealing 1 1/2-inch-long (almost 4 cm) canines. Peccaries eat tubers, roots, seeds, and fruits, and their canines interlock when used for breaking hard seeds so they don't dislocate their jaws. The canines are used in self-defense and communication too. Mouth sounds, such as clicks and clacks, warn the other animals in the group of possible danger. This morning the peccaries stay at the water hole for a few noisy sips and slip back into the forest.

Collared peccaries are hog-like mammals that travel through Santa Rosa's forests in social groups of two to fifteen animals, or even more. Their gray-white collars distinguish them from their rarer, white-lipped cousins.

SENDERO
TURAL,
ATURE PATH

▌ he coati band is now ready to leave the water hole to begin its day of foraging for food. Coatis search for insects, fruits, and small animals that hide in the leaf litter of the forest floor. But they also adapt to what's available, dry season or wet. Since the dry season is the time of the first flowering of many kinds of trees, coatis consume a good quantity of fruits and seeds as they develop. And because coatis sometimes eat fruits without crushing the seeds, they help spread seeds to new parts of the park.

A tired white-faced monkey rests, draped over a tree limb. Monkey troops eat small-seeded fruits and then disperse the seeds by the thousands as they range through the park. Sometimes, however, they chew open immature fruits and destroy the seeds before they develop.

The magpie jay is usually part of a band of many jays. Noisy squabbles erupt when a band defends its territory from other jays.

17

The anole lizard, another dry forest resident, is prey for the coati.

By now, midmorning glare makes it difficult to see. The water hole lies at the bottom of a nearly dry riverbed. A short distance away stands a huge, haunted-looking evergreen tree with a twisted trunk and vines clinging to its limbs. White-faced monkeys sit motionless in the tree's highest branches, legs dangling, apparently asleep. Doves and magpie jays roost in the tree and on the vines, then swoop down to steal sips of water. Tiny anole lizards make acrobatic leaps into the air. They lunge after insects as if hurled from a trampoline.

As the coatis move away from the water hole, one of the young females notices a swarm of army ants smothering some nearby rocks. The remains of a scorpion are being readied for a trip back to the ants' home. Sometimes the ants move as one large mass. Then suddenly the army breaks into columns and sends soldiers out on patrol. First are the scouts. They drag a special abdominal gland along the ground, leaving a scented trail. The next column is made up of workers who follow the trail the scouts have left behind.

But grasshoppers—not ants—are the real reason for the coati's attention. Trying to avoid the ant swarm, the grasshoppers jump frantically from their

Over 150 species of army ants live in the American tropics. These ants form huge colonies of 30,000 to a million creatures or more. Their wolf-pack swarms send insects and larger animals scurrying for safety.

In a search-and-destroy mission, army-ant scouts trace lines over the rocks. Almost no territory is safe from them as some species can hunt to the tops of trees as well as along the forest floor. When the army ants go on patrol, everything in their path is swept out of hiding, including grasshoppers.

● After months without rain, the Sendero Natural is dry and dusty. Along the path are two Indio desnudo, or gumbo limbo, trees with orange-colored trunks. Plant cells beneath the Indio desnudo's peeling bark capture the sun's energy and convert it into sugars and starches to nourish the tree.

hiding places in the leaves and become easy prey for the hungry young coati. At first it has them all to itself, but soon the other coatis rush in to grab a share of the feast.

Coatis don't like to share their food. As each newcomer muscles in, the others growl their protests and try to chase it away. The squabbling continues until the last grasshopper has been consumed.

The grasshoppers have provided a morning meal, but now the coatis move on to explore different hunting grounds. They climb up a ledge of rocks toward a nature path called Sendero Natural. The Santa Rosa Park rangers have created this trail for human visitors to pass through the forest, but sometimes the animals use it too. The dry, desert-colored trail is a sharp reminder of the effect two months without rain can have on a forest.

There aren't any sand dunes here, as there are in the deserts of the African Sahara. Instead there are many plants and animals that have adapted to the scarcity of water. The deciduous trees lose most of their foliage during the dry season, to retain as much water as possible. Layers of their leaves are spread over the forest floor. Without leaves to provide the chlorophyll for photosynthesis, these nonevergreen trees survive by going into a state of dormancy, or sleep. They use the food stored in their roots as sugar and starch until the rains return. Evergreen trees similarly slow down their life processes, to use as little energy as possible.

As the coatis cross the Sendero they pass under a leafless tree with peculiar peeling orange bark. This Indio desnudo ("naked Indian") tree survives the five to six months of the dry season through a special adaptation. Beneath its peeling orange exterior is a base of green bark containing photosynthetic plant cells that capture light. Its trunk is like a giant cylindrical leaf. Farmers plant Indio desnudos to form living fence posts that surround and protect their land.

This morning, the Indio desnudo's remaining fruits have attracted a band of howler monkeys. Clumps of the monkeys hang from the tree's bare branches like Christmas tree ornaments. The howlers announce their presence to the coatis passing below with a brief flurry of throaty roars, then busy themselves with the fruit.

At this time of year, the Indio desnudo tree usually attracts only white-faced monkeys and squirrels. But today, the howlers are supplementing their usual leaf diet with green fruit. By doing so, they too may help disperse this tree's seeds. As the monkeys travel to different parts of their home range, they carry the seeds they've eaten in their guts. Later they defecate in another part of the forest. There the seeds may sprout into trees—if mice and other rodents don't pulverize them first.

As they pass under the tree, the coatis take advantage of fruits howlers have dropped to the ground. What they're looking for, however, are the brightly colored lizards hidden under the litter of leaves.

Coatis are at home on the ground or in the trees. As the young coatis search for lizards on the forest floor, two of the adult females climb into the

● Howler monkeys are named for the roar adult males use to communicate with other howlers and warn away intruders. They live on a diet of leaves, flowers, and fruit. The kind of howler found in Santa Rosa ranges from southern Mexico to northwestern South America.

trees to try their luck there. One tree they avoid, however, is the ant acacia tree. Acacia ants and the acacia tree form one of the forest's many symbiotic, or cooperative, relationships. Each partner gives something and gets something in return.

Most plant leaves have bitter or poisonous chemicals in their leaves. The leaves of the acacia tree, however, are sweet and tasty, a little like some kinds of lettuce. They taste good not only to people; many forest animals like them as well. When an animal such as a caterpillar tries to eat the acacia's leaves, the resident acacia ants respond with a stinging counterattack. These ants guard the acacia leaves like feverish bullies.

In return the ants get a place to live, protected in burrows they tunnel into the acacia tree's thorns. They also get to feed on tiny food-rich nodules which grow at the tips of the acacia tree's leaves. Acacia ants harvest these "Beltian bodies,"—named for the scientist who first discovered their pur-

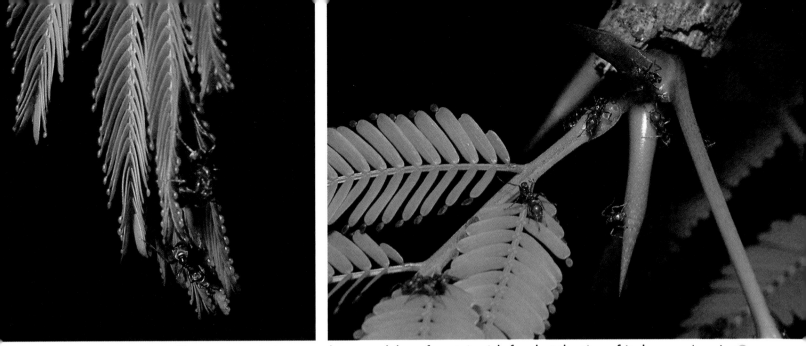

The ant acacia tree produces nodules of protein-rich food at the tips of its leaves. Acacia ants harvest them to feed their young. Acacia ants patrol the leaves of the ant acacia tree, stopping to sip sugary juices from the tree's nectar-secreting glands, visible here as little green volcanoes on the stem of the plant (center of the photo). The nectar glands are one way the tree helps its resident ants, which in turn protect the tree from leaf-eating animals.

A solitary white-faced monkey breaks away from its group to forage on its own.
White-faced monkeys usually give birth to a single offspring in the dry season.

pose—to feed to their developing larvae, or young. Another benefit for the ants is the sugary juice they lick from small glands at the base of the leaves.

The coati and most other animals stay away from the ant acacia tree. But some animals have adapted to the stinging ants, and use the ants' defensive ferocity to their own advantage. A pair of rufous-naped wrens are busy building a nest in the middle of the tree. This nest will serve as a shelter for sleep and rest. The ants get used to the nest quickly and ignore that part of the tree, leaving the birds protected and undisturbed. Then, at the start of the rainy season, the same mated pair of wrens will build a separate nest in the acacia to serve as nursery for their eggs and developing young. The mother wren will remain here to incubate its eggs while the male returns to the first nest.

But even the ant and the acacia's strong mutual-defense system has weak links—as proven by one member of another troop of white-faced monkeys. The monkeys arrive chattering noisily as they leap from one tree to another in search of food. One medium-size male moves away from the group foraging in the treetops. It climbs down a tree standing next to an ant acacia tree, reaches over to one of the acacia's horizontal limbs, and snaps it off so it falls to the forest floor. The monkey breaks off several more acacia branches and then scampers down to the ground.

Each branch has a large thorn with an opening where ants are streaming out in a frenzy. The monkey picks up a branch and begins to crack the thorn open with its teeth. By the vigorous shaking of its head and paws, it's clear the monkey is being stung by the ants and doesn't like it. Still, the monkey persists and licks up the ants and their larvae hidden inside the thorn. The monkey next attacks the thorns of the other fallen branches and then goes on its way.

By now the coatis have nearly reached the end of the Sendero Natural, crisscrossing above the trail in the trees and on the ground. This is not their usual place to hunt for food. But today there are few human visitors around and they have been lucky in finding food. They pass a clearing where the park historical museum is located, and catch a glimpse of a small white-tailed deer feeding on shrubs. Its mother is not far behind, busy in its own search for food. They may have visited the water hole the coatis used earlier in the day.

The white-tailed deer was once hunted for its skin and meat. Under park protection, the population is now slowly recovering.

NOON
AT THE RAINTREE

The park's museum was planned for human visitors, but the large trees near it attract the animals. One especially large tree here is called a raintree because insects feed on its sap, which then passes through their bodies to rain down on the ground below. The raintree is at the edge of an open field, bordered by an old stone-fenced pasture, but coatis risk exposure for a rest on the tree's broad limbs. By now they are panting like dogs in the morning heat.

For the last two months of the dry season, from about March to April, the raintree's branches are full of fruits and flowers. This attracts the creatures who pass by daily to reach the water hole. White-faced monkeys, howler

The raintree near the park museum is an occasional roosting spot for the forest's birds and other wildlife. The tree is related to the guanacaste tree and is native to the dry lowlands of Costa Rica. The raintree's flowers are pollinated by night-visiting moths.

Leaf-cutter ants carry pieces of leaves back to their underground nest which holds as many as five million worker ants. The ants use the leaf fragments to fertilize an underground fungus garden that is the ant colony's source of food.

monkeys, and brilliantly colored birds called trogons often make rest stops at the raintree. The tree is a source of food, a trellis on which other plants find support, a halfway station for long-distance flyers, and a shade tree for over-heated visitors.

Monkeys feed on its flowers and fruits. Moths carry pollen to its flowers at night. Leaf-cutter ants snip pieces off its leaves and carry them away to underground nests. Bristling cactus plants and delicate orchid flowers adorn the tree's immense spreading branches, and plants called bromeliads, relatives of the pineapple, hang everywhere from its limbs. Even the hollow cavities created when tree limbs break off and fall to the ground are useful—they provide sleeping places for ctenosaur lizards, relatives of the iguana.

One of the two-year-old coatis discovers a trail of leaf-cutter ants meandering down the trunk of the raintree and leading off into the woods. Coatis don't usually hunt leaf cutters as food because they are spiny and hard to digest. But this young coati still watches curiously as the worker leaf cutters stream double-time before it, climbing over and under any obstructions in their path. They carry precious leaf fragments from the raintree back to a nest in the ground, where they add the leaves to a kind of fungus garden.

Inside the ants' nest, another group of workers clean the leaf pieces, removing bacteria and other unwanted growth, and then chew them into smaller parts. Mixed with saliva and feces, the ground-up leaves become fertilizer for the underground fungus garden—thousands of tiny plants that look like beads or miniature mushrooms. The mushrooms will feed the queen ant, the builder of the nest, as well as the nearly five million workers.

While the young coati watches the ants, the other coatis begin climbing into the raintree for a midday rest. As they climb, they hear a sudden clatter of sharp claws on the bark, and a gray blur crashes into the grass below. Their invasion has alarmed a large male ctenosaur that was basking on a tree limb in the early afternoon sun. Now the lizard will move off to find a new patch of sun in a nearby open field. Ctenosaurs are cold-blooded; they depend on the sun's heat to keep their bodies warm.

The ctenosaur begins to bob its head. It seems a curious behavior, but it serves a purpose. Twenty feet (7 m) off to the east, another male ctenosaur begins bobbing as well. Each is sending out a warning to other male ctenosaurs: "Stay away, stay away. Find somewhere else to stay."

Near the raintree stands an equally large guanacaste tree. Together the trees mark two corners of what was once a cattle corral. Although few cattle come here anymore, workhorses from the park's administration center visit to feed on the ear-shaped fruit of the guanacaste tree. Today two of them are busy chewing up guanacaste and raintree fruits, ignoring the other animals around them.

The feeding on the guanacaste and raintree by animals such as monkeys, peccaries, and leaf-cutter ants does not always help the forest grow. For a tree to spread its seeds—for a tree to help make a forest—it needs consumers to transport its seeds. But by the time many of these forest animals are finished eating the fruit, there is nothing left of the seeds. Powerful teeth have crushed them to powder. Fortunately, cattle and free-ranging horses come to the rescue. These seed consumers sometimes swallow seeds whole, and then wander off to deposit them, undigested, some distance away from the parent tree.

An adult male ctenosaur basks in the warmth of the sun. Ctenosaurs are related to the iguana and are found in open fields, savannas, and other dry areas. Young ctenosaurs eat insects; adults prefer a diet of leaves.

MIDAFTERNOON
PARK BOUNDARY

By midafternoon the temperature reaches 85°F (29.4°C), and despite their rest period the coatis are dehydrated and in need of water. They now set out for a different water hole, about a mile (almost 2 km) from the first. In the distance the Orosi volcano is wrapped in a wreath of clouds. Thanks to the efforts of Santa Rosa Park planners, the volcano and the slope of forest leading up to it are now included in the area of protected park.

On their way, the coatis cross a field of jaragua grass. When cattle ranchers owned this area that is now parkland, they introduced the tall jaragua

The Orosi volcano (in the background, behind a mass of clouds) and the lands leading up to it are now included within a protected park district called Guanacaste National Park. The enlarged district safeguards animals that move beyond the limits of Santa Rosa during the driest months to reach higher elevations near the volcano.
Below: The fruits on this gourd tree growing in a field of jaragua grass stay on its branches for about seven months before turning yellow-green and falling off. Free-ranging horses then eat the seed-rich pulp and disperse the seeds through the park.

grass into fields they had cleared of trees. Now part of the park, these grasslands show signs of returning to forestland again. The gourd tree the coatis pass is an encouraging example. Its large fruits are a favorite food for range horses. They break open the hard outer shell with their teeth and swallow seed-rich fruit pulp, often with little chewing. This gourd tree is probably growing where it is thanks to horses.

The jaragua field leads directly to the entrance to the park and the highway beyond it. From here there is a glimpse of what is happening to land not protected by the park. Along the road are long stretches of fenced-in pastureland and farmhouses. As the coatis pass close to the edge of the field, one of the adults suddenly begins to bark and runs for the nearest tree. Its cries of distress signal the rest of the band to follow. They are alarmed by the appearance of a cattleman riding a horse near the paved road. A mare and its colt trail behind.

The horseman skirts the fields of specially irrigated land which provide grass for large herds of brahma cattle. Thanks to the wisdom of the park managers, the forest and privately owned pasture exist side by side. The land best suited for cattle is preserved for farm use. The land that is not suited for farming is being turned into a wildlife park.

Brahma or cebu cattle are bred on pasture land in Guanacaste Province, the location of Santa Rosa National Park. The park territory and separate pastures and farmlands will be preserved, each serving its own important function.

Fires threaten the renewal of the tropical dry forest. Cattle ranchers set fire to their fields to burn off unwanted shrubs and to produce ash that fertilizes the soil for new grass needed as cattle feed. But fire in Santa Rosa can destroy years of new tree growth and delay the rebirth of the forest.

ON THE WAY TO THE SECOND WATER HOLE

As the coati band moves away from the road and the entrance to the park, the mother of the three adolescent coatis notices that one is missing. Young male coatis begin to establish their independence at about the age of two. Before the rainy season arrives, the young males will strike off on their own and spend most of the rest of their lives as solitary wanderers. They will join bands like the one they grew up in only during the mating seasons, when they will father children of their own.

The loud, shrill chittering the coati mother hears coming from the base of a nearby tree, however, is a sign that the young male didn't just wander off. The young coati is in a struggle for its life. A large boa constrictor has seized the youngster with its sharp teeth and powerful jaws and is beginning to coil its 6-foot-long (2 m) body around it.

The coati band rushes onto the scene in response to the youngster's cries. Together the six coatis paw and bite at the snake, trying to find a vulnerable spot in its thick skin. If they can get at the boa's head before the boa tucks it inside its protective coils, they might have a chance to save the youngster. But the snake has moved quickly and the coatis can't force it to release its viselike grip.

In minutes, the young coati is lifeless. Sensing there is nothing more they can do and that they too are in danger, they move quickly off into the bush. The surviving coatis are all unhurt, but their struggle with the snake has made the need for water even more urgent.

The boa constrictor, a nonvenomous snake, captures its prey with sharp, curved teeth and squeezes it to death. Boas are thought to seek out a good spot and wait for a lizard, bird, or mammal up to the size of a young deer to come along.

THE AFTERNOON WATER HOLE

In the northwest end of Santa Rosa National Park there is a river that, at this dry time of year, is reduced to one or two pools of water. Soon even these will disappear. As the summer sun begins to sink, the coatis cross a dusty path along the riverbank. They are not alone in their search for water. A distinctive scent and tooth clicks and grumblings signal the presence of peccaries. These peccaries, however, are not the kind the coatis usually meet.

White-lipped peccaries are rare in Santa Rosa. In the dry season, they come down from the forested slopes of the volcanoes in search of food. When they find a good supply of tree fruits, they settle in for a feast. But now, food is not their concern. Thirty peccaries are squirming, rooting and squealing with delight in a ragged pool of brown water and decaying leaves. Their presence means the park offers enough wilderness and space to attract animals that had once moved out to find larger, more hospitable lands.

The coatis and the peccaries could share the water hole, but for the moment the coatis keep a safe distance and watch from up in the trees. As the last of the peccaries drinks its fill, a noise from the forest scares them into squealing, hair-bristling bunches. The herd moves quickly away over a large fallen tree, but the little newborns can't get over the log. Back come the mothers to urge them on. The now silent peccaries trail off in single file.

Whatever made the noise in the forest seems to be gone. The coatis approach the water hole. One takes a sip, then backs off with a bark when a river turtle suddenly appears. As the turtle's shell sinks into the muddy waters, everything becomes quiet and the coatis can at last satisfy their thirst.

In the dry season, the water hole is reduced to a small pool filled with leaves and mud. Two weeks later there may be no water at all. The photograph on page 42 shows the water hole in the wet season.

up and seldom swallow them whole. But sometimes agoutis gather more fruits than they can eat and bury some for another day. Many buried fruits are lost or forgotten, and their seeds may sprout to produce part of the next generation of trees.

The sun is nearly setting as the coatis take a last drink and then seek shelter in the high branches of the same fig tree they had slept in the night before. With darkness, new sounds ring out through the forest. While one set of animals retires for the evening, another group begins to stir. The forest floor is alive with animals creeping and crawling—and sometimes running for their lives. Through the night air whoosh squadrons of bats that keep up a steady stream of reconnaissance flights until sunrise. They are probably fruit bats, which find their food by odor, not by the echolocation method used by insect-eating bats. The fruit bats are major seed dispersers in the forest. Each one is a kind of flying Johnny Appleseed, leaving seed-filled droppings everywhere.

The dim forms of white-faced monkeys appear in a nearby tree. They too have settled in for the night. While the mother coati keeps a watch on the monkeys, it grooms the fur on its remaining young male's back. The young coati chitters softly—a kind of high-pitched whistle—and curls its tail in front of its face. The young female settles in beside the mother. The monkeys are the last things the coatis see as they drift off into sleep, safely nestled in the vines of the tree.

White-lipped peccaries, named for the wash of white hairs around their snouts, travel in large groups, often of thirty or more, and need extensive areas of wilderness to survive.

At the end of each day, the coatis seek out a tree to serve as their home for the night.

WET SEASON

Nearly five months have passed since the coati band spent its mornings and afternoons shuttling from one dry-season water hole to another. July is several months into the rainy season, and the forest has changed from desert brown to luxuriant green. Trees that were once nearly empty of leaves are now thick with foliage, flowers, and fruits. Insects that had all but disappeared are now visible on nearly every plant and shrub. The water hole close to where the young coati was eaten by the snake is now a continuously flowing river. And the small band of coatis has changed, also.

In wet season, the water hole becomes a free-flowing river.

In contrast to the dry season colors of desert brown, the wet season in Santa Rosa, from about May to November, offers a glorious array of greens.

The fig tree, here displaying wet-season foliage, marks the entrance to the Sendero Natural—the nature trail.

Thorn bugs, or treehoppers, are among the thousands of insects that appear when wet season rains begin. Thorn bugs are attentive parents, protecting their eggs and their young from predators until they are adults. Caterpillars (bottom) are especially visible in the wet season. The bristles on its coat are for protection and discourage most predators.

The childless female coati has given birth to two males. The mother of the two males and the female has now added two infant females to its family. But it is about to lose its remaining son; as expected, it is leaving its mother and the other coatis to go off and live as a solitary male.

The newly mature young male heads toward the lowlands to the south. The coati travels alone, at times crossing a road used by horses and park vehicles. The path winds through an open field of jaragua grass and past the gourd tree its family had visited in the dry season. The grass is high and green, the earth is slippery with mud, and the sky is thick with rain. A single white-tailed deer fawn grazes in the grass at the side of the path. The deer pays little attention until the coati is almost on top of it. Only then does the deer move quietly to the cover of the woods.

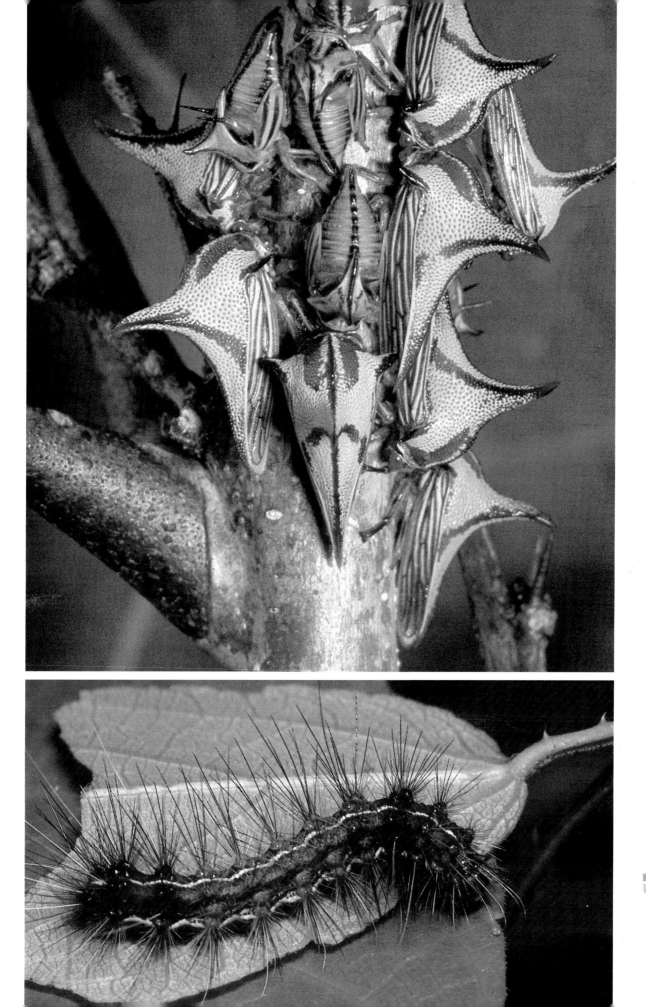

When the first few sprinkles of rain fall through the canopy of nearby trees, the howler monkeys roar as if in protest. Their fierce calls allow them to communicate with other howler monkeys, and are also a response to lightning, rain, and the presence of humans.

By late afternoon, there is a break in the rains that have soaked the forest for almost two hours. The coati has spent part of the time nestled near the trunk of a tree. Now, as it goes deeper into the forest, it passes a rare sight—a tapir wallowing alone in a huge pool of water. Tapirs are shy, long-snouted mammals the size of ponies. In the wet season they stuff their bellies with all the leaves they need. Tapirs love to sit and loll in water holes at any time of the year.

The young coati lets the tapir have the water hole to itself. The coati can get its water from pools in the trunks of trees or caught in depressions in the forest floor. It climbs a nearby tree. Using the sharp claws of its front and back feet, it walks upside down along a huge, nearly horizontal limb to reach some appetizing fruits. Acrobatics like this are not unusual for coatis, which use their long tails to help them balance. Its stomach filled, the young coati ends its first day of travel on its own by curling into sleep in a crotch of the same tree that provided its supper.

The tropical dry forest can be restored from seeds in tree fruits like these. The poro-poro pod (top, left) and other yellow pods (top, right) ripen and burst open to release their seeds. Wind distributes the shiny brown pods (bottom, left). The ear-shaped fruits of the guanacaste tree (bottom, right) fall to the ground where they rot and split open, or are eaten by animals.

A Baird's tapir lounges in a water hole. This largest living land mammal native to Central America is an endangered species because of overhunting.

INT● 〰 THE FUTURE

Two days and 7 miles (12 km) farther south, the solitary coati reaches a deserted beach that stretches 3 miles (5 km) long. This will be its home for most of the next year. It will continue to travel on its own. It will forage for a diet of crabs and turtle eggs. During the mating season—in Santa Rosa that is the beginning of the dry season—it will seek out a band of coati females and young just like the one it grew up in.

At first, it may be chased off by a competing male already accepted in a breeding territory. But it will try its luck with each new band of coatis it meets until it is finally accepted. It will mate, and then it will leave the band again to continue life on its own.

The coati's tail is nearly half as long as its body. Although the tail does not serve as an additional limb, as a monkey's does, the coati uses it for balance while climbing in the forest trees.

Naranjo beach marks the western boundary of Santa Rosa National Park. Naranjo and the neighboring Nancite beach are sites for the yearly nesting rituals of the Pacific ridley sea turtle.

EPIL●GUE

A year has passed in Santa Rosa National Park. This view of the daily life of a small band of coatis offers a way to appreciate and understand a world that was almost lost. To rebuild the forest will require help from the park rangers and scientists who must fight fires and plant trees; it will depend on the survival of plants, and on animals (like the coatis) that will disperse the forest's seeds. The new forest will take hundreds of years to grow. But the wait will be worth it.

"For most tropical peoples, wildlands are the closest there will ever be to libraries, concert halls, museums, universities, parks, and sports arenas."

"What direct goods have the tropics provided? For a start, chickens, eggs, elephants, turkeys, beef, pryrethrum, corn, rice, coffee, corsage orchids, tea, chocolate, morphine, tobacco, cocaine, dahlias, cotton, marijuana, aquarium fish, marigolds, strychnine, parrots, bamboo, macadamia nuts, rum, pepper, honey bees, vanilla, milk, peppers, cinnamon, dates, quinine, rubber, gardenias, bananas, avocados, mahogany, pineapples, impatiens, humans, sorghum, rosewood, coconuts, Brazil nuts, peanuts, potatoes, sweet potatoes, tapioca, squash, chimpanzees, pumpkins, beans, cane sugar, molasses, tomatoes, cats, guinea pigs, citrus, white rats, palm oil, rhesus monkeys. How many polio victims realize that their vaccine was grown in a chicken egg, and chickens are nothing more than tropical pheasants specialized at preying on bamboo seed crops (which an Illinois farmer mimics with his chicken feed)."

From "The Future of Tropical Ecology" by Daniel H. Janzen, Professor of Biology, University of Pennsylvania.

Alejandro Marin, son of Santa Rosa National Park administrator Sigifredo Marin, holds seeds that may produce 60-foot- (20-m) tall guanacaste trees. The seeds are collected under parent trees, sprouted in nursery pots, and later planted in the forest.

The flowers of the poro poro tree and many other trees appear in the dry season. When the poro poro's seeds mature, they are carried off by the wind to take root, if they are lucky.

Glossary

acacia ant (ah-KAY-shah) a species of stinging ant, about ¼-inch (6 mm) long, that makes nests inside ant-acacia tree thorns

acacia trees (ah-KAY-shah) a large group of woody plants, related to peas and beans, that are common in most warm countries. A few species, called ant acacia trees, produce pairs of large sharp thorns that house acacia ants.

agouti (uh-GOO-tee) a tropical rodent about the size of a large house cat, but much stockier; a relative of the guinea pig

anole (UH-nohl) also called anolis lizard, a small, active member of the iguana family of lizards; typically about 5 inches (13 cm) long, including their tails

army ants ants that form nomadic armies of worker and soldier ants in the service of a queen ant. Their prey consists of insects, small vertebrates such as lizards and frogs, and occasional baby birds. There are at least 150 species of army ants in the American tropics.

Beltian bodies (BELT-shun) tiny protein-rich nodules that grow at the tips of ant acacia leaflets to provide food for acacia ants

boa constrictor a large, tropical snake that kills by constricting, or squeezing, its prey

bromeliads (bro-MEE-LEE-adz) tropical plants in the pineapple family which often grow on tree trunks or branches. Most bromeliads are epiphytes.

chlorophyll the green coloring matter in plants, necessary for photosynthesis

coati (koh-AH-tee) a tropical mammal related to the raccoon, with a range from Arizona and New Mexico to Argentina

ctenosaur (TEEN-uh-sore) a large, primarily vegetable-eating lizard that resembles the iguana and is a skilled burrower and tree climber

deciduous tree (di-SID-you-us) a tree that sheds its leaves annually, in contrast to an evergreen tree. The red oak is an example of a deciduous tree.

epiphyte (EP-if-fight) a plant that grows on trees or other plants. Many epiphytes absorb moisture directly from the air.

fungus garden (FUHN-gus) a garden of mushroom-like plants that leaf-cutter ants grow in underground nests. The fungus garden provides the ants' only food.

gomphotheres (GOME-foh-thayres) extinct mastodon-like animals that are thought to have ranged through North America and Central America from 10,000 to 60,000 years ago

guanacaste tree (gwa-nuh-KAS-tee) a tropical American tree, native from Mexico to Brazil, introduced worldwide

howler monkeys monkeys named for the howling roar they use to mark their territory, and to communicate among themselves. The six species of howlers in the American tropics live in groups of males, females, and associated juveniles and infants.

Indio desnudo (IN-dee-oh des-NUDE-oh) the Spanish name for the tree called the naked Indian tree for its reddish-brown bark. While leafless in the dry season in Santa Rosa, it is capable of photosynthesis because of living plant cells under its bark.

jaragua grass (ha-RAH-gwa) a kind of tall pasture grass brought from tropical Africa and introduced to Costa Rica about 1943

leaf-cutter ant a kind of ant that uses leaf fragments cut from trees to nourish its underground fungus garden. There are over 200 kinds of leaf-cutter ants worldwide.

magpie jay   a tropical relative of the North American blue jay, the magpie jay lives in social groups and eats fruits, insects, seeds, and many other foods.

morpho butterfly (MORE-foh) a large, tropical butterfly with spectacular blue color on the upper surface of its wings, but with duller coloration and eye spots on the underside of the wings. "The bluest thing in the world," according to one scientist.

musk   a liquid of strong odor, secreted from a special gland in certain animals and used to mark their territories

peccary (PECK-cah-ree) social mammals which are related to domestic pigs

photosynthesis   (foh-toe-SIHN-thuh-sis) a process by which green plants use sunlight, carbon dioxide, and water to manufacture sugar

puma (POO-mah)   a long-tailed member of the cat family found in North, Central, and South America; also called a mountain lion.

Quebrada El Duende   the name of a Santa Rosa National Park water hole. The Spanish words can be roughly translated as "The Troll's Creek."

sloths   tree-dwelling tropical mammals named for their slow movement through tree canopies in search of leaves to eat

tapir (TAY-per) large hooved mammal about the size of a small pony, related to horses and rhinoceroses. Tapirs have flexible snouts and feed on leaves, fruits, and seeds.

territory   the area an individual or group of animals defends against other animals, especially members of their own species

trogan (TRO-gun)   a tropical and subtropical bird. Males are colored iridescent green with blue on their heads and red or yellow breasts.

tropical dry forest   a kind of tropical forest with an extended rainless season, in contrast to tropical rain and cloud forests. This dry season makes it, in many ways, a kind of temporary desert. Dry tropical forests used to be the most extensive kind of tropical forest in the world until they were cut down for farming, ranching, and other development. Tropical dry forests are not as diverse as rain forests (with 40–90 percent fewer tree species), but are much more diverse than typical temperate forests.

tropical rain forest   a humid evergreen forest found at low elevation in regions between the Tropics of Cancer and Capricorn. Tropical rain forests have abundant rainfall and warm temperatures through the year. Cloud forests are another kind of humid tropical forest that occur at high elevations.

For Further Reading

BOOKS FOR YOUNG READERS

Baker, Jeannie. *Where the Forest Meets the Sea*. New York: Greenwillow Books, 1987.

Dorros, Arthur. *Rain Forest Secrets*. New York: Scholastic Inc., 1991.

Forsyth, Adrian. *Journey Through a Tropical Jungle*. New York: Simon & Schuster, 1989. This book describes life in Costa Rica's Monteverde cloud forest.

Landau, Elaine. *Tropical Rain Forests Around the World*. New York: Franklin Watts, 1990.

Miller, Christina. *Jungle Rescue: Saving the New World Tropical Rain Forests*. New York: Atheneum, 1991.

Mitchell, Arthur. *Wildlife of the Rainforest*. New York: Oxford Scientific Films, Mallard Press, 1990. Photographic presentation of rain forest wildlife.

Pringle, Laurence. *Living Treasure—Saving Earth's Threatened Biodiversity*. New York: Morrow Junior Books, 1991.

GENERAL REFERENCE BOOKS

Caufield, C. *In the Rainforest*. Chicago: University of Chicago Press, 1984.

Collins, Mark, ed. *The Last Rain Forests—A World Conservation Atlas*. New York: Oxford University Press, 1990.

Forsyth, Adrian, and Ken Miyata. *Tropical Nature: Life and Death in the Rain Forests of Central and South America*. New York: Charles Scribner's Sons, 1987.

Head, Suzanne, and Robert Heinzman, eds. *Lessons of the Rain Forest*. San Francisco: Sierra Club Book, 1990.

Janzen, Daniel H., ed. *Costa Rican Natural History*. Chicago: The University of Chicago Press, 1983. The best single source book for understanding the dry forest and all forests throughout Costa Rica.

Wilson, E.O. *Biodiversity*. Washington, D.C.: National Academy Press, 1988.

MAGAZINE AND JOURNAL ARTICLES

Two of the best general magazine articles are:
Lessem, Don. "From Bugs to Boas, Dan Janzen Bags the Rich Coast's Life." *Smithsonian*, Dec 1986.

Lewis, Thomas. "Dan Janzen's Dry Idea: Time, Wind and the Animals Will Restore Costa Rica's Dry Forest." *International Wildlife*, Jan–Feb 1989.

To find technical articles on Santa Rosa National Park and Costa Rica, see:
Janzen, Dan, ed. *Costa Rican Natural History*, listed under General Reference Books.

For information about the coati, see:
Kaufmann, John. "Ecology and Social Behavior of the Coati, *Nasua narica*, on Barro Colorado Island, Panama." University of California Publications in Zoology, 60: (95–222), 1962.

Index

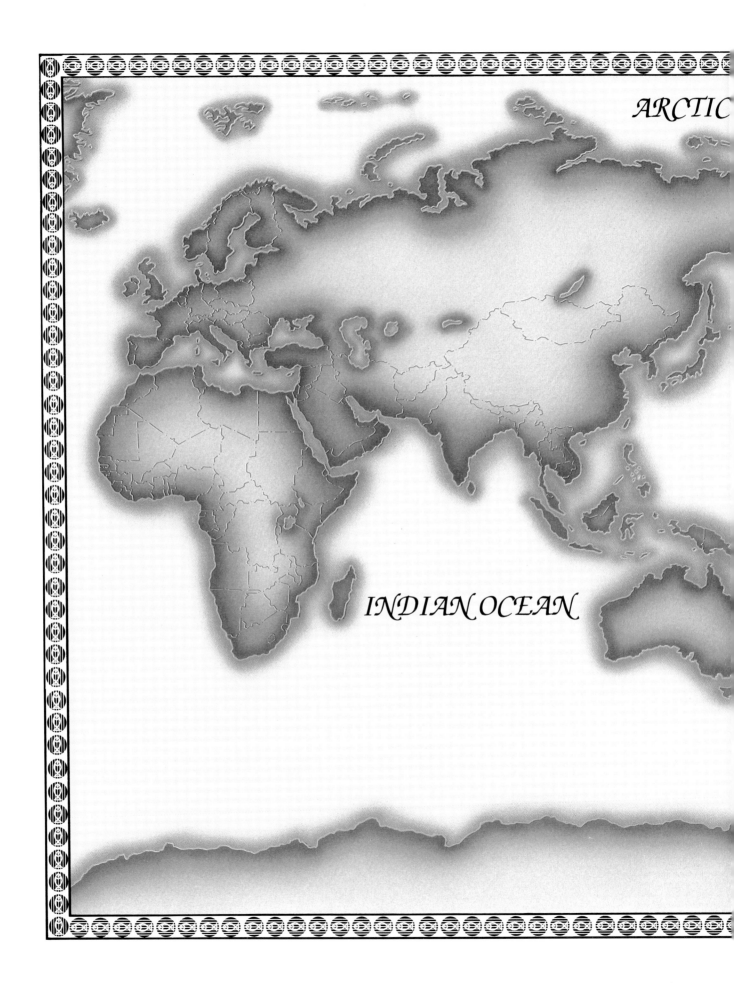

ARCTIC

INDIAN OCEAN

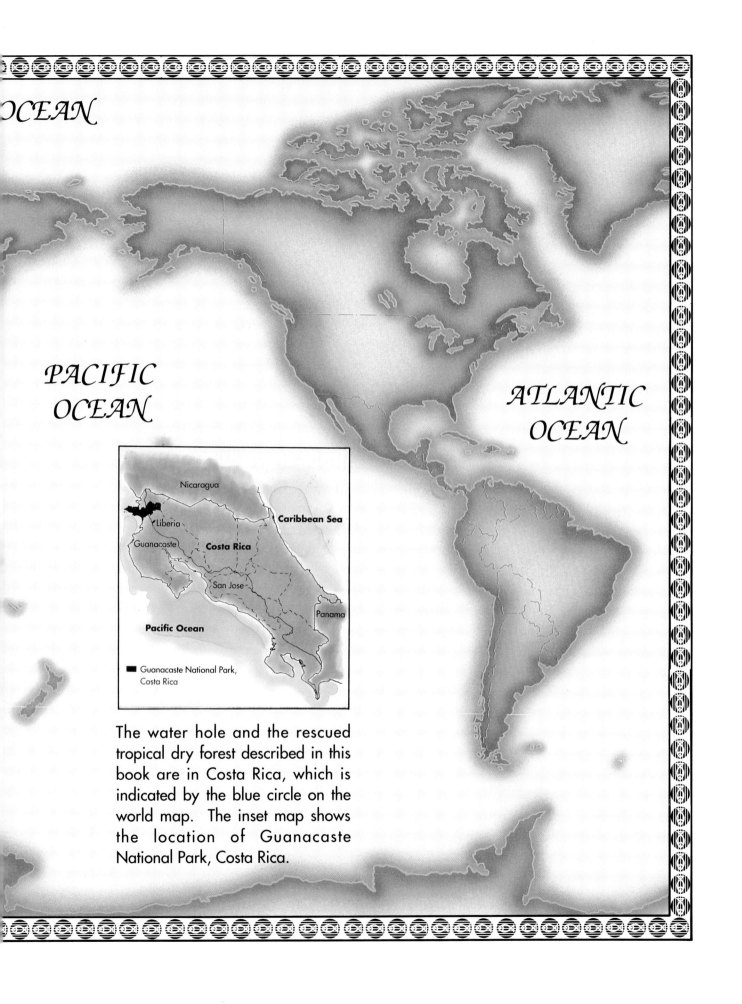

OCEAN

PACIFIC
OCEAN

ATLANTIC
OCEAN

Nicaragua

Liberia

Caribbean Sea

Guanacaste

Costa Rica

San Jose

Panama

Pacific Ocean

Guanacaste National Park,
Costa Rica

The water hole and the rescued
tropical dry forest described in this
book are in Costa Rica, which is
indicated by the blue circle on the
world map. The inset map shows
the location of Guanacaste
National Park, Costa Rica.